DAILY LIFE

in
~•~ Ancient Greece ~•~

by Lisa M. Bolt Simons

Consultant:
Jonathan M. Hall
Phyllis Fay Horton Distinguished Service Professor
in the Humanities
The University of Chicago

CAPSTONE PRESS
a capstone imprint

First Facts are published by Capstone Press,
1710 Roe Crest Drive, North Mankato, Minnesota 56003
www.capstonepub.com

Library of Congress Cataloging-in-Publication Data

Simons, Lisa M. B., 1969–
Daily life in ancient Greece / Lisa M. Bolt Simons.
pages cm.—(Ancient Greece)
Includes bibliographical references and index.
ISBN 978-1-4914-0272-6 (library binding)
ISBN 978-1-4914-0277-1 (eBook PDF)
Summary: "Describes life at home, education, careers, and other characteristics of daily life
for the ancient Greeks."—Provided by publisher.
1. Greece—Social life and customs—Juvenile literature. I. Title.
DF77.S467 2015
938—dc23   2013049253

Editorial Credits

Aaron Sautter, editor; Bobbie Nuytten, designer; Svetlana Zhurkin, media researcher;
Jennifer Walker, production specialist

Photo Credits

Alamy: Mary Evans Picture Library, 13, North Wind Picture Archives, 9, 11, 19, 21;
National Geographic Creative: H.M. Herget, cover (top), 7, 15; Newscom: Universal
Images Group/Leemage, 14; Shutterstock: Arkady Chubykin, cover (bottom), 1,
Dhoxax, 8, Emi Cristea, 18, Ensuper (paper), back cover and throughout, ilolab (grunge
background), cover, 1, James Steidl, 20, Kamira, back cover (bottom right), Madlen, 12,
Maxim Kostenko (background), 2 and throughout, mexrix, 5 (back), Roberto Castillo
(column), back cover and throughout; Wikipedia: MatthiasKabel/Sting, 17;
XNR Productions, 5 (map)

Printed in China by Nordica
0414/CA21400593
032014   008095NORDF14

TABLE OF CONTENTS

GROWING UP
IN ANCIENT GREECE

Imagine growing up in Greece 3,000 years ago. You wake up on a mattress filled with grass or feathers. If you're a boy, you may go to school. If you're a girl, a **tutor** teaches you at home instead. During free time you can play with your toys. These include clay figures, wax dolls, or balls made from pig bladders. Welcome to life in ancient Greece!

FACT:

Students often did school work on a wooden tablet that was filled with wax. They wrote on the wax with a bone or metal **stylus**. The wax could be smoothed out to erase the work and continue writing.

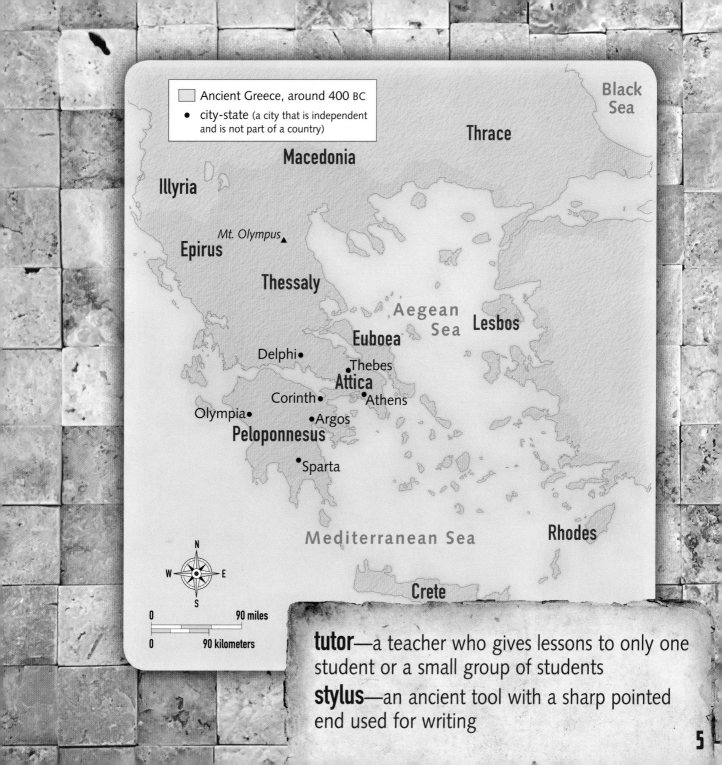

Ancient Greece, around 400 BC

• city-state (a city that is independent and is not part of a country)

Black Sea

Thrace

Macedonia

Illyria

Mt. Olympus ▲

Epirus

Thessaly

Aegean Sea

Lesbos

Euboea

Delphi •

Thebes •

Attica

Corinth •

• Athens

Olympia •

• Argos

Peloponnesus

• Sparta

Mediterranean Sea

Rhodes

Crete

N
W   E
S

0   90 miles

0   90 kilometers

tutor—a teacher who gives lessons to only one student or a small group of students

stylus—an ancient tool with a sharp pointed end used for writing

5

Whether **wealthy** or poor, people's lives were busy in ancient Greece. Children in wealthy families usually went to school or were taught at home. But poor families usually made children do chores at home instead. Men fought in the army or had jobs outside the home. Most women stayed home to care for their houses or manage the family's **slaves**.

A FATHER'S DECISION

Greek fathers could choose to accept or reject a newborn baby. If he named the baby within 10 days of its birth, it became part of the family. But if he rejected the baby, it was often placed in a clay pot and left by the road. A different family could then adopt the baby.

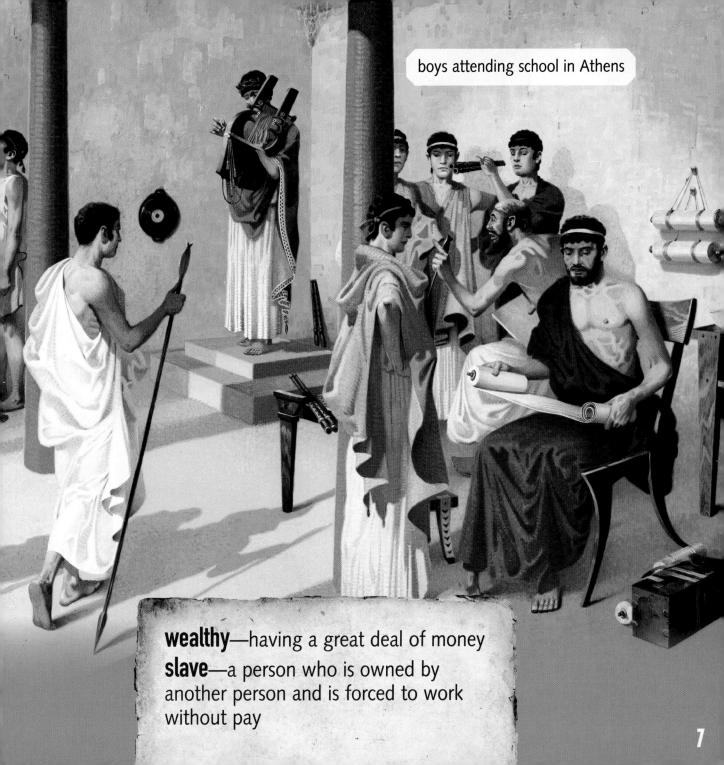

boys attending school in Athens

wealthy—having a great deal of money
slave—a person who is owned by
another person and is forced to work
without pay

LIFE AT HOME

Clothing

Most families in ancient Greece made their own clothes. Everyone wore free-flowing clothes called **tunics**. Cloaks were also worn in cold weather. At first nearly everybody's clothes were white. But people began wearing brightly colored clothing around 500 BC. Some people wore strapped sandals or boots to protect their feet, but many walked barefoot.

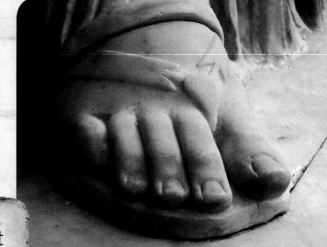

tunic—a loose sleeveless garment

The ancient Greeks often wore colorful, loose-fitting clothing.

Houses

Ancient Greek houses were made of wood, mud bricks, or stone. Two or three rooms were built around a **courtyard**. Men, women, and children had separate rooms. Every house had an altar for making animal **sacrifices** to the gods. Most houses didn't have a bathroom. People instead used **chamber pots** or went outside.

courtyard—an open area surrounded by walls
sacrifice—an offering made to a god
chamber pot—a type of bowl that people used as a toilet

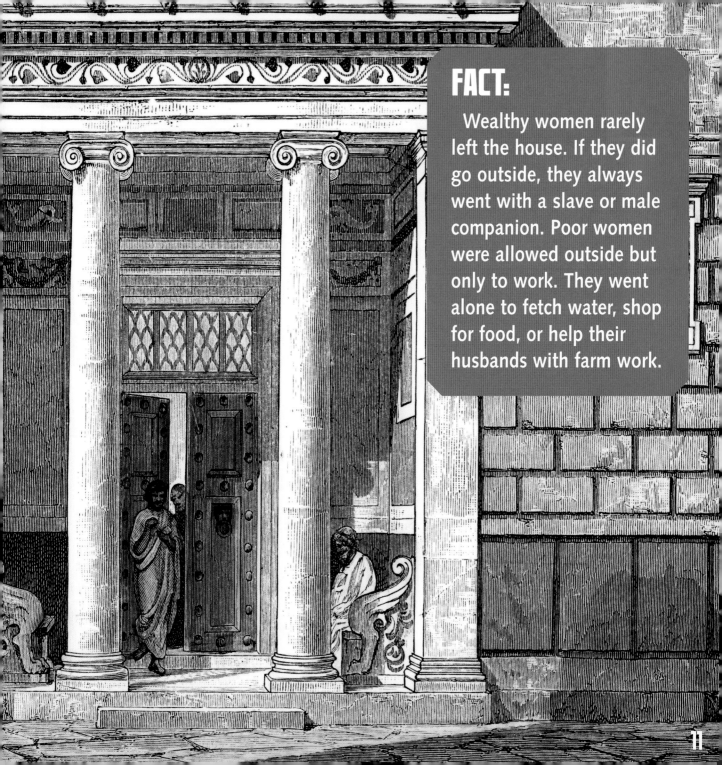

Food

The ancient Greeks ate three meals a day. Fish and seafood were popular. People also ate a lot of bread, fruit, garlic, and onions. Much of the food was cooked in olive oil. People ate their food with their fingers. They usually drank water or wine mixed with water.

THE IMPORTANT OLIVE TREE

Olive trees were very important to the ancient Greeks. Greeks often ate olives. They used olive oil for cooking, lighting lamps, and making skin care products. Olive oil was also sold to other countries. Olympic winners' crowns were even made of olive tree leaves woven together.

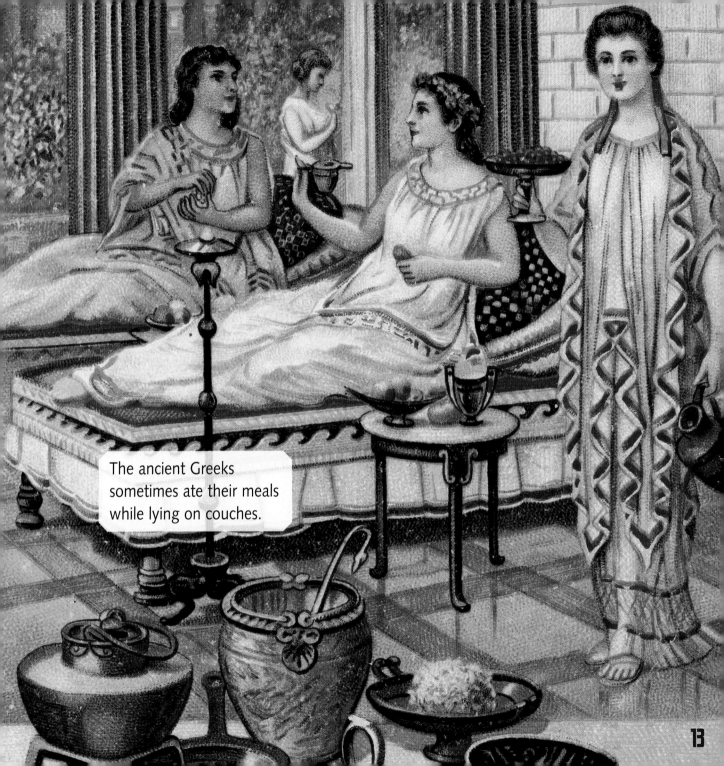

The ancient Greeks sometimes ate their meals while lying on couches.

13

EDUCATION AND WORK

Work

Greek men were expected to work outside the home. Many served in the military. Others worked as fishermen, farmers, **craftsmen**, or artists. Farmers grew crops such as barley and wheat in fields close to home. Craftsmen worked in shops around the **agora**.

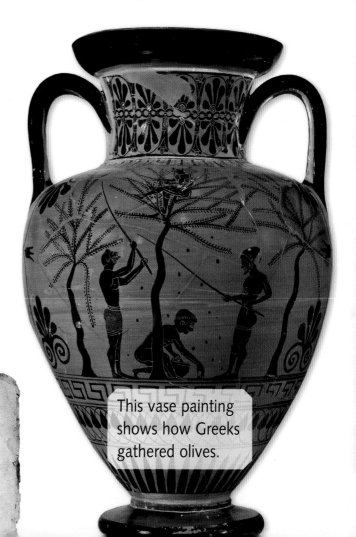

This vase painting shows how Greeks gathered olives.

craftsmen—people who are skilled at making things with their hands

agora—an open marketplace in ancient Greece

Military Education in Sparta

Most young Greek men went to military school at age 18. They trained to be soldiers or sailors in the navy. They prepared for battles that often happened between Greek **city-states**.

Military training was especially tough in the city-state of Sparta. Boys were sent to live at military schools at age 7. They trained very hard and had little food or clothing, no shoes, and hard beds. Young men took a fitness test between the ages of 18 and 20. If someone didn't pass, he was no longer considered a citizen of Sparta.

city-state—a city that is independent and is not part of a country

large square sails to provide speed on open ocean

120 feet (37 meters) long

200 crew members, including rowers

Ancient Greek Trireme

170 oars on three levels

RELIGION AND THE ARTS

Honoring the Gods

Religion was a big part of ancient Greek life. The Greeks believed in many gods. Many large temples were built for the gods. Each temple honored a certain god and included a statue of the god inside. The Greeks often performed animal sacrifices and held other **ceremonies** to please their gods.

ceremony—special actions, words, or music performed to mark an important event

temple for Greek god Hephaestus

statue of Greek goddess Athena

Arts and Entertainment

The ancient Greeks enjoyed several forms of entertainment. They danced, sang, and played instruments such as **lyres**. The Greeks built large open-air theaters into hillsides. They performed plays in the theaters to honor the gods. Singers and poets also told tales of Greek heroes and gods for audiences at the theaters.

lyre—a small, stringed, harplike instrument

a theater in ancient Athens

Glossary

agora (uh-GOHR-uh)—an open marketplace in ancient Greece

ceremony (SAYR-uh-moh-nee)—special actions, words, or music performed to mark an important event

chamber pot (CHAYM-buhr POT)—a type of bowl that people used as a toilet in the past

city–state (SI-tee-STAYT)—a city that is independent and is not part of a country

courtyard (KORT-yard)—an open area surrounded by walls

craftsmen (KRAFTS-men)—people who are skilled at making things with their hands

lyre (LIRE)—a small, stringed, harplike instrument

sacrifice (SAK-ruh-fisse)—an offering made to a god

slave (SLAYV)—a person who is owned by another person and is forced to work without pay

stylus (STY-luhs)—an ancient tool with a sharp pointed end used for writing

tunic (TOO-nik)—a loose sleeveless garment

tutor (TOO-tur)—a teacher who gives lessons to only one student or a small group of students

wealthy (WELL-thee)—having a great deal of money

Read More

Macdonald, Fiona. *You Wouldn't Want to be a Slave in Ancient Greece!: A Life You'd Rather Not Have*. You Wouldn't Want To. New York: Franklin Watts, an imprint of Scholastic Inc., 2014.

Macdonald, Fiona. *I Wonder Why Greeks Built Temples and Other Questions About Ancient Greece*. I Wonder Why. New York: Kingfisher, 2012.

Steele, Phillip. *Ancient Greece*. Navigators. New York: Kingfisher, 2011.

Internet Sites

FactHound offers a safe, fun way to find Internet sites related to this book. All of the sites on FactHound have been researched by our staff.

Here's all you do:

Visit *www.facthound.com*

Type in this code: 9781491402726

 **Super-cool stuff!** Check out projects, games and lots more at **www.capstonekids.com**

Critical Thinking Using the Common Core

1. The ancient Greeks believed in many gods. Name three ways in which they honored and worshiped the gods. (Key Ideas and Details)

2. Why do you think boys in Sparta went to live at tough military schools at such a young age? (Integration of Knowledge and Ideas)

Index